Natural Resources

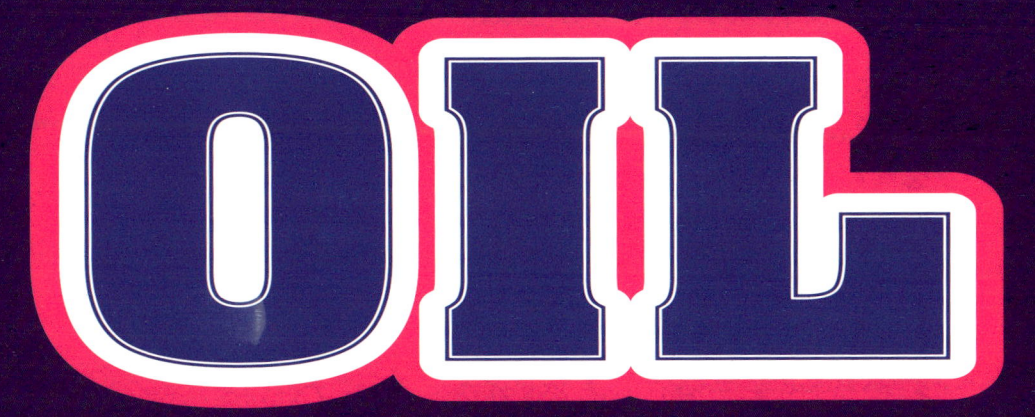

OIL

Jason McClure and John Willis

LIGHTBOX
openlightbox.com

LIGHTBOX

Go to **www.openlightbox.com** and enter this book's unique code.

ACCESS CODE

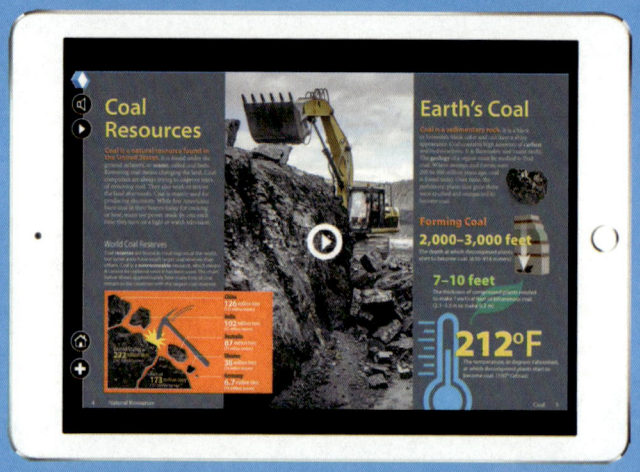

LBS34568

Lightbox is an all-inclusive digital solution for the teaching and learning of curriculum topics in an original, groundbreaking way. Lightbox is based on National Curriculum Standards.

STANDARD FEATURES OF LIGHTBOX

AUDIO High-quality narration using text-to-speech system

VIDEOS Embedded high-definition video clips

ACTIVITIES Printable PDFs that can be emailed and graded

WEBLINKS Curated links to external, child-safe resources

SLIDESHOWS Pictorial overviews of key concepts

TRANSPARENCIES Step-by-step layering of maps, diagrams, charts, and timelines

INTERACTIVE MAPS Interactive maps and aerial satellite imagery

QUIZZES Ten multiple choice questions that are automatically graded and emailed for teacher assessment

KEY WORDS Matching key concepts to their definitions

Copyright © 2017 Smartbook Media Inc. All rights reserved.

Natural Resources

CONTENTS

2 Lightbox Access Code
4 Oil Resources
5 Earth's Oil
6 Oil in the United States
8 Oil Products
9 Oil as Fuel
10 Making Gasoline
12 Oil as Power
13 Heating Homes
14 The Oil Industry
15 Oil Imports
16 Technology in the Gulf
18 Managing Oil
20 Oil Industry Jobs
21 Quiz
22 Activity
23 Key Words/Index
24 Log on to www.openlightbox.com

Oil Resources

Oil companies set up towers called derricks over wells. These structures help to support and stabilize the drilling equipment.

Oil is one of the most important natural resources in the United States. It is found underground in rock and sand. Oil is a fuel. It is used to power everything from cars and airplanes to houses and cities. Oil is in demand all over the world. Countries without oil rely on countries that have oil to provide it to them. However, accessing oil creates problems for the environment. Oil companies keep searching for new ways to find oil that does not hurt the environment.

How Oil is Formed

Oil is a **fossil fuel**. It takes millions of years for it to form.

Plants and animals die and sink to the sea floor.

Layers of dirt and sediment cover the remains.

Heat and pressure turn the remains into fossil fuels, including oil.

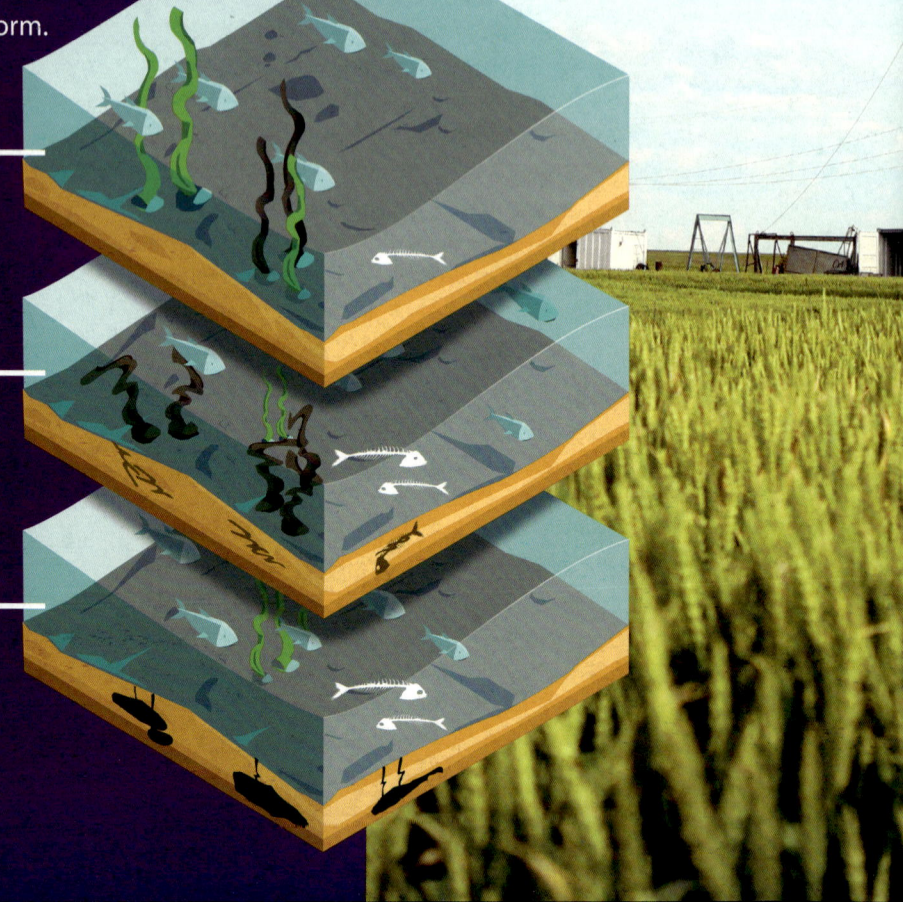

Natural Resources

Earth's Oil

Where oil is found depends on the geology of an area. **Crude oil** is found in places where there was animal and plant life hundreds of millions of years ago. Most organisms that became oil lived in the ocean. Areas such as Saudi Arabia and Texas were under water hundreds of millions of years ago. These waters were full of marine animal and plant life. Those animals and plants died and became part of the underlying earth. Today, those areas contain much of the world's oil.

World Oil Reserves

Oil is found in large amounts in many places around the world. However, oil is a **nonrenewable** resource. It cannot be replaced once it is used. This chart shows how many barrels of oil each oil-rich country is estimated to have in their **reserves**.

Saudi Arabia
262.6 billion barrels

Venezuela
211.2 billion barrels

Canada
175.2 billion barrels

Iran
137 billion barrels

Kuwait
104 billion barrels

United Arab Emirates
98 billion barrels

Russia
60 billion barrels

Oil 5

Oil in the United States

Oil has been produced in 31 states in the United States and in the waters off of its coasts. Most of the oil produced in the United States comes from Texas, North Dakota, California, Alaska, and Oklahoma.

Approximately 17 percent of U.S. oil is produced by offshore oil wells. Almost all of this oil production takes place in the Gulf of Mexico. Some oil platforms can drill for oil in water depths of more than 10,000 feet (3,048 meters).

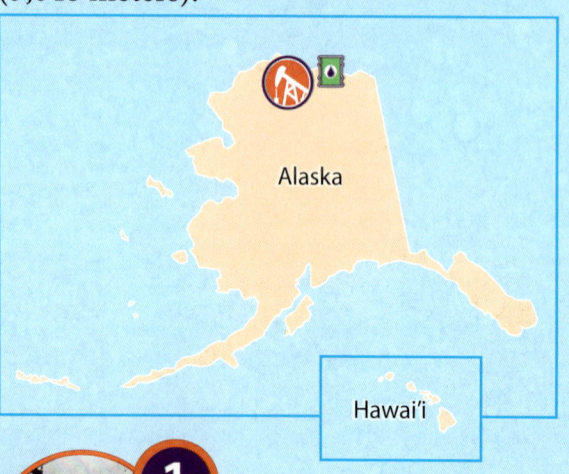

1. Spindletop, Beaumont, Texas. On January 10, 1901, the first oil field on the Gulf Coast was found. By the end of 1902, there were more than 500 oil companies operating in the area.

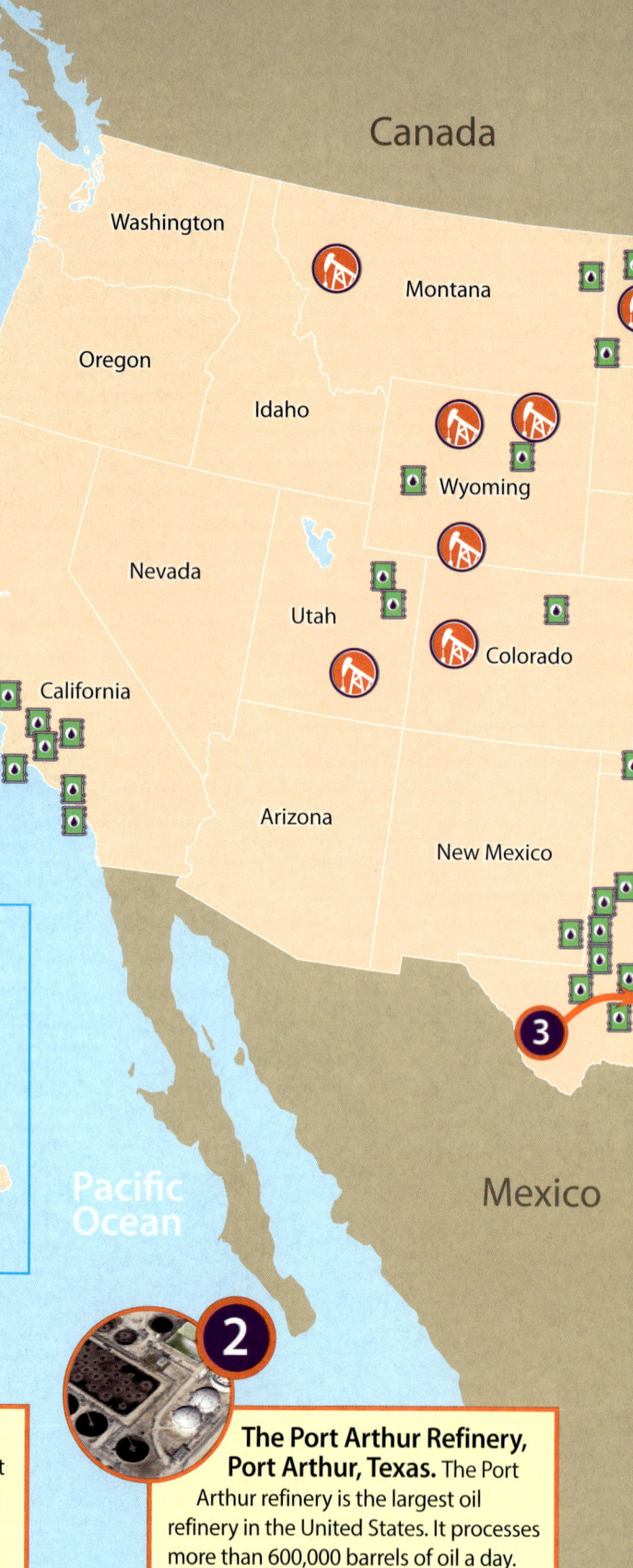

2. The Port Arthur Refinery, Port Arthur, Texas. The Port Arthur refinery is the largest oil refinery in the United States. It processes more than 600,000 barrels of oil a day.

6   Natural Resources

MAP LEGEND
- Producing Oil Fields
- Potential Oil Fields
- United States
- Other Countries
- Water

Santa Rita No. 1, Big Lake, Texas. In 1923, the University of Texas struck oil on land that it owned in West Texas with its discovery well, *Santa Rita No. 1*. This well, along with others built in the area, made the University of Texas one of the wealthiest U.S. schools.

Oil 7

In 2015, gasoline accounted for 45 percent of the petroleum products made in U.S. refineries.

Oil Products

The crude oil that is found in the United States has many uses.
Oil provides heat for homes and power to run factories. It also provides the raw materials to make **petrochemicals** and plastics. However, most oil is used for powering cars. In North America, two-thirds of all oil is used for transportation.

Products Made with Oil
Oil is used to make a wide variety of products from plastic bottles to laundry detergents.

Computers

Sneakers

OIL

Cameras

Soccer Balls

8   Natural Resources

Oil as Fuel

In 2014, there were more than one billion cars on roads worldwide. Most of these vehicles require gasoline to operate. Gasoline is made from oil. To make gasoline, companies take oil and **refine** it. This means they separate the ingredients that make up the oil. One of these ingredients is gasoline. Crude oil is the source of other fuels as well.

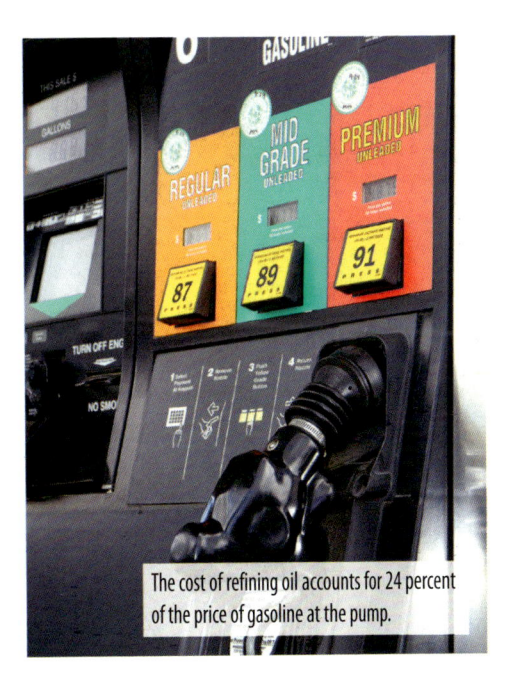

The cost of refining oil accounts for 24 percent of the price of gasoline at the pump.

Where Does a Barrel of Oil Go?

Oil is often stored in large metal containers called barrels. A barrel holds 42 gallons (159 liters) of oil. These 42 gallons can make approximately 45 gallons (170 L) of oil-based products.

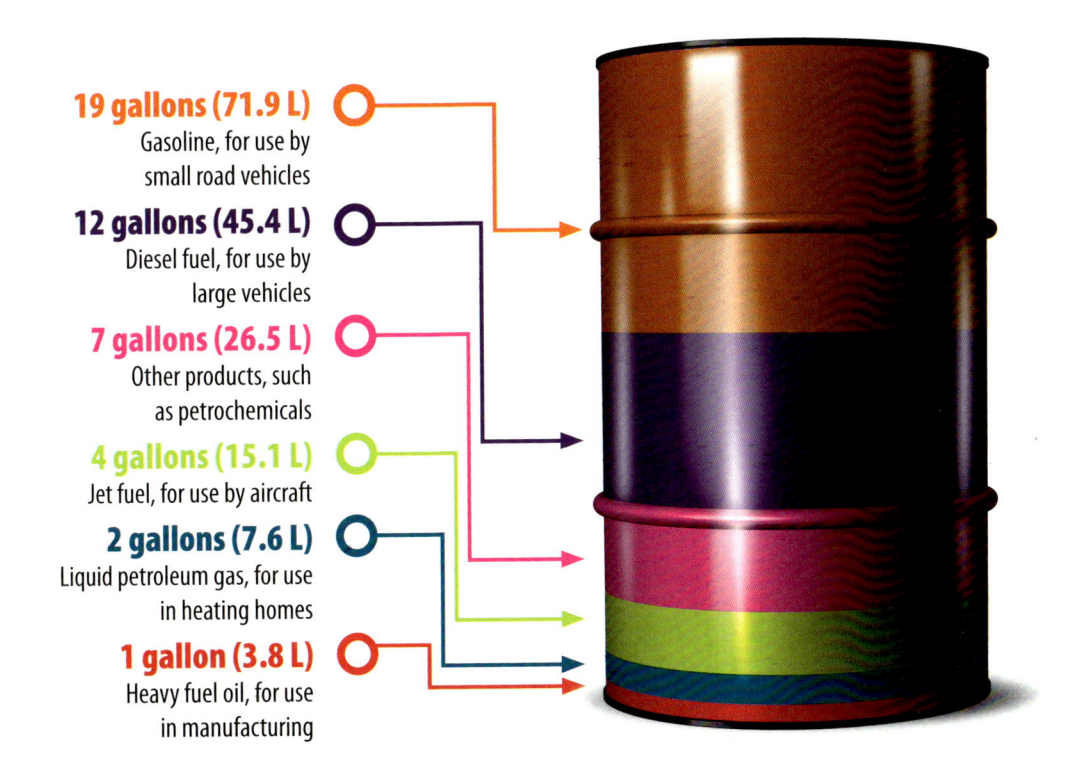

19 gallons (71.9 L)
Gasoline, for use by small road vehicles

12 gallons (45.4 L)
Diesel fuel, for use by large vehicles

7 gallons (26.5 L)
Other products, such as petrochemicals

4 gallons (15.1 L)
Jet fuel, for use by aircraft

2 gallons (7.6 L)
Liquid petroleum gas, for use in heating homes

1 gallon (3.8 L)
Heavy fuel oil, for use in manufacturing

In the past 30 years, U.S. gasoline production has increased by 53 percent.

Making Gasoline

Making gasoline is a long process. First, the crude oil is removed from the ground. It then is moved to a refinery. There, the gasoline is separated from the crude oil and made ready for use.

10 Natural Resources

Producing Gasoline

Finding Oil
Scientists drill for cores, or samples, of rock deep underground. The scientists study these cores to see if the conditions might be present for oil to have formed.

1

Drilling Oil
Once oil is found, drilling machines are set up. They drill into the ground toward the oil source. When the drilling reaches the oil, the oil is pumped to the surface.

2

Transporting Oil
The oil then has to be shipped to the refinery for processing. If the oil is mixed with sand, it is shipped by truck. If it is in a liquid state, it travels through a pipeline to the refinery.

3

Processing Oil
When crude oil arrives at the refinery, it is heated in furnaces. The heat separates and turns it into the different fuels. Gasoline goes through a treatment process to get it ready for use.

4

Storing Oil
The gasoline is placed in large storage tanks. When it has been sold, it is shipped to customers by pipeline.

5

Oil 11

Oil as Power

Oil provides power for more than cars. Industry uses oil as an energy source as well. The type of oil that industry uses for energy is called heavy oil. Heavy oil is not refined like gasoline. It is thick and contains more **pollutants**. Oil companies use heavy oil to make gasoline. It is burned to create the heat needed in the oil refining process. Other industries that rely on heavy oil to create heat include the pulp and paper industry and the electricity industry.

In 2015, liquid petroleum generated more than 17 million megawatts of energy in the United States.

Oil Use by Industry

In the United States, oil is used for a variety of purposes. This use can include powering vehicles and generating electricity. Although most of the oil in the United States is used for transportation, it contributes to other sectors as well.

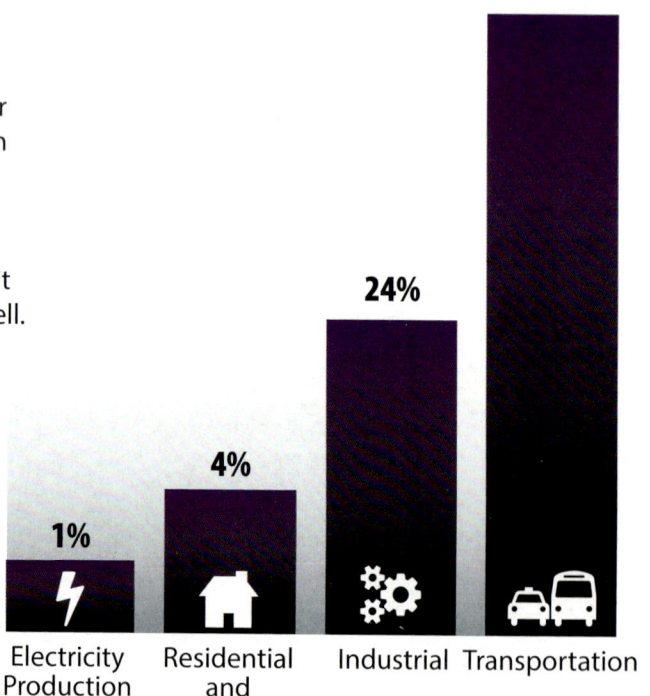

- 1% Electricity Production
- 4% Residential and Commercial
- 24% Industrial
- 71% Transportation

Natural Resources

Heating Homes

In winter, many people in the United States use oil to heat their homes. Oil is known to provide the hottest flame of any fossil fuel. This means that it heats up an area faster than other forms of energy. Heating oil is used mostly in the Northeast, in states such as New York and Pennsylvania. The number of houses that use heating oil has declined by 41.5 percent since 1984. Today, most homes use electricity or natural gas for heating.

About 80 percent of the 6.2 million households in the United States that rely on heating oil to heat their homes are found in the Northeast.

Oil Consumption by Country

The United States is the top consumer of oil in the world. In 2014, the United States used approximately 19 million barrels of oil per day. In contrast, South Korea used only 2.3 million barrels per day in 2014.

Country	Daily Oil Use (million barrels)
United States	19.0
China	10.7
Japan	4.4
India	3.7
Russia	3.1
Saudi Arabia	2.9
Brazil	2.8
Germany	2.4
Canada	2.4
South Korea	2.3

Daily oil use for 2014, in millions of barrels.

Oil

Every summer in the United States, gas prices increase by as much as 15 cents per gallon (3.8 liters).

The Oil Industry

Oil production is part of the energy industry. This industry also includes natural gas and electricity production. The energy industry contributes greatly to the economy of the United States. In 2011 alone, the industry made more than $1 trillion. This was about 8 percent of all the goods and services sold in the United States that year.

The Price of Gasoline

The price of gasoline depends on the cost of the crude oil. However, there are other costs involved, too. The oil must be refined. It must be transported. It must be sold with advertising. Finally, governments add to the cost of gasoline by charging taxes. All of these factors contribute to the final cost of gasoline.

- Transportation & Advertising
- Refining
- Taxes
- Price of Crude Oil

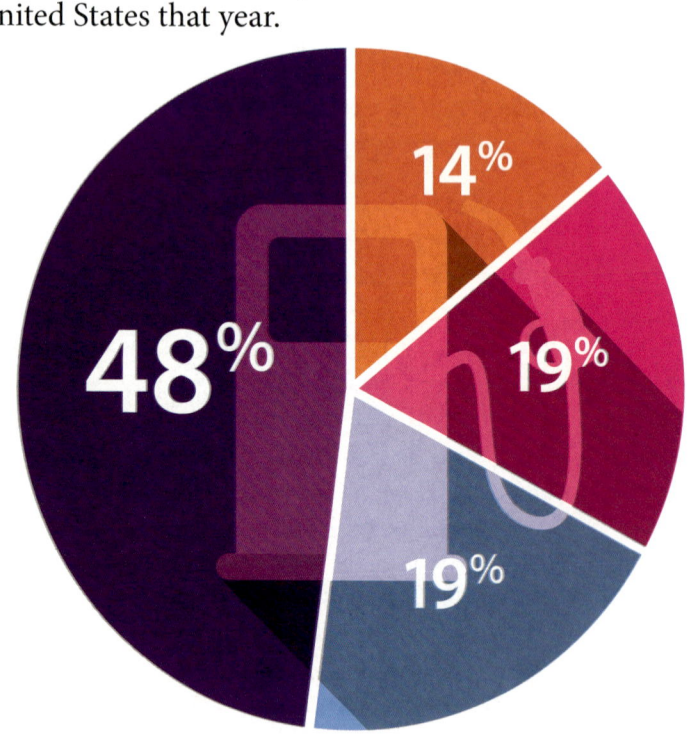

14%
19%
19%
48%

14 Natural Resources

Oil Imports

The United States uses more oil than it produces, even though it is the third-largest crude oil producer in the world. The country **imports** the nearly 27 percent of the oil that it uses. These imports come from Canada, Saudi Arabia, Venezuela, and other countries. The countries the United States buys oil from are decided by the U.S. government as part of its global policy.

Since 1994, U.S. oil imports from the Middle East have decreased, while Canadian imports have increased by nearly 300 percent.

The Pipeline Network

Canada provides nearly 40 percent of oil imports to the United States. Pipelines transport most of this oil. Pipelines are considered the safest and most efficient way to move oil from one place to another. There are over 250,000 miles (402,336 kilometers) of pipeline in the United States and Canada.

Pipelines in the United States and Canada

Map Legend
- Major Pipelines
- United States
- Canada
- Mexico

Oil 15

Technology in the Gulf

The oil industry depends on technology in many ways.
Oil can be buried deep under the ocean. Technology is used to find and remove it. Oil companies must try not to hurt the environment. This, too, requires special technologies. Keeping the **extraction** process safe for people is important as well.

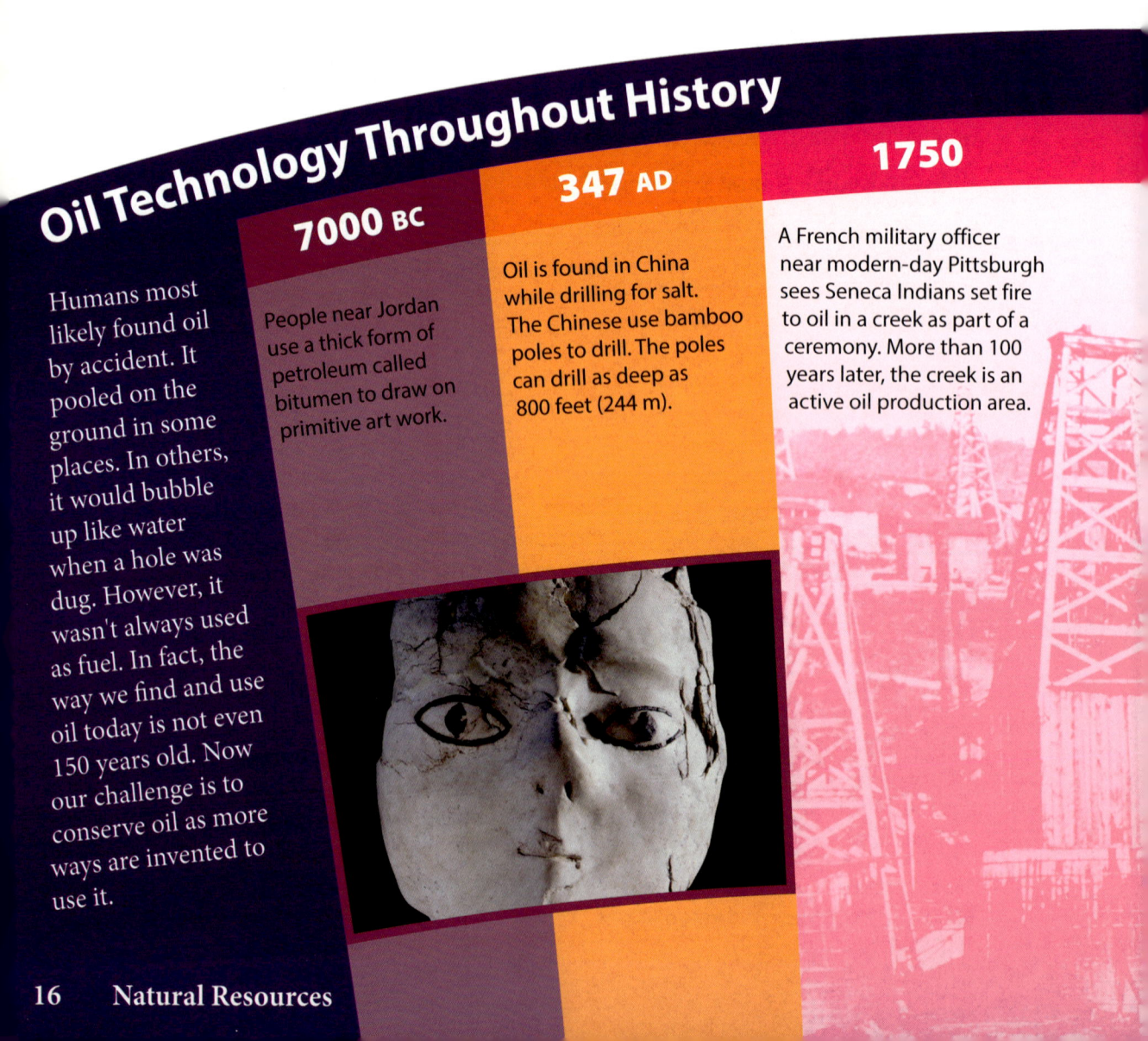

Oil Technology Throughout History

7000 BC
Humans most likely found oil by accident. It pooled on the ground in some places. In others, it would bubble up like water when a hole was dug. However, it wasn't always used as fuel. In fact, the way we find and use oil today is not even 150 years old. Now our challenge is to conserve oil as more ways are invented to use it.

People near Jordan use a thick form of petroleum called bitumen to draw on primitive art work.

347 AD
Oil is found in China while drilling for salt. The Chinese use bamboo poles to drill. The poles can drill as deep as 800 feet (244 m).

1750
A French military officer near modern-day Pittsburgh sees Seneca Indians set fire to oil in a creek as part of a ceremony. More than 100 years later, the creek is an active oil production area.

16 Natural Resources

When a rich source of oil is found under the ocean, a permanent oil platform is built over it. The type of platform depends on the depth of the well. Fixed platforms are used when the water is up to 1,500 feet (457 m) deep. Spar platforms are used in water up to 10,000 feet (3,048 m) deep.

Drilling for oil on a floating platform in the ocean is dangerous for people and the environment. The Deepwater Horizon oil rig, built in 2001 off the south east coast of Louisiana, was the deepest in history at 30,050 feet (10,683 m). In April 2010, the rig exploded into the Gulf of Mexico. Eleven people lost their lives. The rig sank and oil began to leak out of the well. It took six months to seal the leak. More than 4 million barrels of oil spilled into the Gulf of Mexico during that time. It was the largest oil spill in history.

1827
British geologist John Crawford reports seeing an oil field in Burma. He estimates that it produces 300,000 barrels a year. The oil is used in that region for lighting and boat building.

1859
The first oil well in the United States is drilled near Titusville, Pennsylvania. The drill was homemade by Edwin L. Drake. His efforts to drill for oil were laughed at by many. After his success, however, the drilling method he invented started the U.S. oil industry.

1886
The first automobile to run on gasoline is invented. The inventors are Europeans Karl Benz and Wilhelm Daimler. The machine is called the Benz Patent Motorwagon.

2016
New technologies are invented every year that burn fuel for transportation and electricity. Some scientists say that oil will eventually run out. Governments and environmental groups work to find ways to cut down on the use of oil. They also make efforts to educate people about the limited supply of oil.

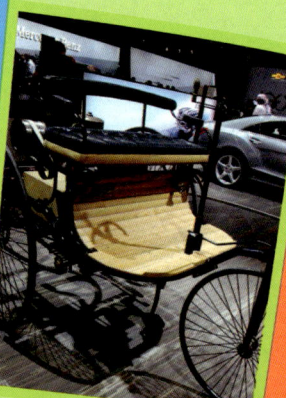

International law grants every country the exclusive right to drill for oil within 200 miles (322 km) of its coastline.

Managing Oil

Oil is a resource people use for many things. However, getting the oil can damage the environment. Forests might be removed to build an oil drilling plant. Mountains might be blasted. The plant and animal life in these places might be harmed by the processes used to find and extract oil.

Producing oil also affects the quality of the air. Oil refineries make **greenhouse gases**, which cause climate change. Many governments and advocacy groups work with oil companies to protect the environment, both in the United States and around the world. They also work to ensure that U.S. oil resources are used properly.

Natural Resources

Governments
Governments set rules that guide how and where oil companies can work. These rules tell the companies how big their work site can be and how they must clean any pollution they create. These rules also indicate where drilling is not allowed, such as in protected natural areas.

Individuals
Due to the harm oil development causes the environment, many people are beginning to watch their use of oil and oil products. They try to carpool, walk, or ride bikes more often. Some people are taking action to ensure that oil resources in the United States are being used in a responsible way. They work with environmental groups and governments to make sure oil companies are being as environmentally friendly as possible.

Companies
Oil companies are aware that their work can harm the environment. Many have started programs to restore the land they dig and reduce the amount of greenhouse gases they produce. They hire environmental experts to help them find better ways to access oil. They also invest money and time into finding new extraction methods.

Environmental Groups
Environmental groups work with governments and oil companies to make sure that the companies are following the rules. These groups also look for ecosystems that need to be protected and bring that information to the government and the oil companies. The work of environmental groups helps protect the environment while still allowing oil companies to do their work.

Oil 19

Oil Industry Jobs

There is a wide range of jobs within the oil industry. Each job has different tasks to perform and requires a certain type of training.

Surface Land Agent

Duties: Buys land for oil companies, works with the community to address concerns

Education: 2 years of college training

Surface land agents work with oil companies and communities. Their job is to talk to the people who may be affected by an oil company's work in an area. They also take the concerns of the people to the oil company.

Pipeline Worker

Duties: Monitors pipelines for leaks, repairs problems, and conducts simple tests

Education: High school diploma, on-the-job training

Pipeline workers build giant pipes that carry oil from one place to another. With more than 192,396 miles (309,631 km) of pipelines in the United States, pipeline workers are always busy making sure that pipelines are safe and working properly.

Truck Driver

Duties: Operates large trucks to help remove materials from the work site

Education: Special driver's license

Digging up oil often involves moving a great deal of earth and rock. Oil fields use large dump trucks to carry this material away. To drive such giant trucks, drivers must be very skilled. They train a long time to learn how to operate such big machines safely.

Quiz

1. How much oil does the United States use every day?
2. Which country has the largest estimated oil reserves?
3. How do most people use oil in their daily lives?
4. How many gallons of oil does a barrel hold?
5. What is most oil used for in the United States?
6. Which country is the largest consumer of oil?
7. Which country exports the most oil to the United States?
8. Which offshore oil rig exploded in the Gulf of Mexico in 2010?
9. When did humans first use petroleum?
10. When was the first gasoline-powered automobile invented?

ANSWERS
1 About 19 million barrels 2 Saudi Arabia 3 As fuel for their cars 4 42 gallons 5 Transportation 6 United States 7 Canada 8 Deepwater Horizon 9 7000 BC 10 1886

Oil 21

Make a Lava Lamp

Materials Needed

clear 2-liter plastic bottle

vegetable oil

water and Alka Seltzer tablets

flashlight

food coloring

Oil and water do not mix. This is because oil is less dense, or lighter, than water. Oil floats on top of water. In this activity, use this fact to create your own lava lamp.

1. Fill the bottle about one quarter full of water. Fill the rest of the bottle with the vegetable oil. Let the oil separate from the water and settle.

2. Add a few drops of food coloring. Watch the food coloring settle at the bottom of the bottle. Once the food coloring has settled, break two Alka Seltzer tablets in half and drop them into the bottle.

3. Shine the flashlight through the back to see the lava lamp colors even better. As the Alka Seltzer dissolves, the effect will stop. Add more Alka Seltzer to see it again.

Natural Resources

Key Words

crude oil: a dark, thick oil that has not been refined

extraction: the process or act of obtaining something by pulling or forcing it out

fossil fuel: an energy source formed from the remains of plants and animals that lived long ago

greenhouse gases: any gases that contribute to global warming

imports: brings products or commodities into a country from another country and makes available for purchase

nonrenewable: something unable to be replaced once it is used

petrochemicals: a range of products made from chemicals that are produced during the processing of crude oil

pollutants: waste materials that contaminate the air, land, and water

refine: to improve something by removing unwanted substances from it

reserves: resources known or believed to exist in a certain location

Index

crude oil 5, 8, 9, 10, 11, 12, 14, 15

electricity 12, 13, 14, 17
environment 4, 16, 17, 18, 19

Deepwater Horizon 17, 21

fuel 4, 9, 11, 13, 16, 17, 21

gasoline 8, 9, 10, 11, 12, 14, 17, 21
government 14, 15, 17, 18, 19
greenhouse gases 18, 19

heavy oil 12

ocean 5, 6, 7, 15, 16, 17

pipeline 11, 15, 20
platforms 6, 17

refine 6, 9, 10, 11, 12, 14, 18

technology 16, 17

water 5, 6, 16, 17, 22

Oil   23

LIGHTBOX

➕ SUPPLEMENTARY RESOURCES

Click on the plus icon ➕ found in the bottom left corner of each spread to open additional teacher resources.

- Download and print the book's quizzes and activities
- Access curriculum correlations
- Explore additional web applications that enhance the Lightbox experience

LIGHTBOX DIGITAL TITLES
Packed full of integrated media

VIDEOS

INTERACTIVE MAPS

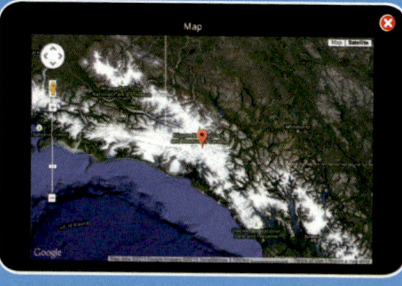

WEBLINKS

SLIDESHOWS

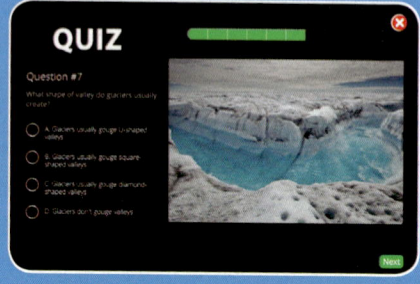

QUIZZES

OPTIMIZED FOR
✓ TABLETS
✓ WHITEBOARDS
✓ COMPUTERS
✓ AND MUCH MORE!

Published by Smartbook Media Inc.
350 5th Avenue, 59th Floor New York, NY 10118
Website: www.openlightbox.com

Copyright © 2017 Smartbook Media Inc.
All rights reserved. No part of this publication may be reproduced, stored in a retrieval system, or transmitted in any form or by any means, electronic, mechanical, photocopying, recording, or otherwise, without the prior written permission of the publisher.

Library of Congress Control Number: 2016931226

ISBN 978-1-5105-1401-0 (hardcover)
ISBN 978-1-5105-1402-7 (multi-user eBook)

Printed in Brainerd, Minnesota, United States
1 2 3 4 5 6 7 8 9 0   20 19 18 17 16

052016
052016

Project Coordinator: Jared Siemens
Art Director: Terry Paulhus

Every reasonable effort has been made to trace ownership and to obtain permission to reprint copyright material. The publisher would be pleased to have any errors or omissions brought to its attention so that they may be corrected in subsequent printings.

The publisher acknowledges Getty Images, iStock, Alamy, and Corbis Images as its primary image suppliers for this title.

24   Natural Resources